T5-CCU-616

DISCARD

JOURNEY TO THE PAST
INVESTIGATING PRIMARY SOURCES

LANDMARKS THROUGHOUT AMERICAN HISTORY

BY MICHAEL RAJCZAK

Gareth Stevens
PUBLISHING

Please visit our website, www.garethstevens.com. For a free color catalog of all our high-quality books, call toll free 1-800-542-2595 or fax 1-877-542-2596.

Library of Congress Cataloging-in-Publication Data

Names: Rajczak, Michael, author.
Title: Landmarks throughout American history / Michael Rajczak.
Description: New York : Gareth Stevens, [2020] | Series: Journey to the past : investigating primary sources | Includes index.
Identifiers: LCCN 2018057200| ISBN 9781538240403 (library bound) | ISBN 9781538240380 (paperback) | ISBN 9781538240397 (6 pack)
Subjects: LCSH: Historic sites--United States--Juvenile literature. | United States--History, Local--Juvenile literature.
Classification: LCC E159 .R335 2020 | DDC 973--dc23
LC record available at https://lccn.loc.gov/2018057200

First Edition

Published in 2020 by
Gareth Stevens Publishing
111 East 14th Street, Suite 349
New York, NY 10003

Designer: Katelyn E. Reynolds
Editor: Jill Keppeler

Photo credits: Cover, pp. 1, 13 (main) Sean Pavone/Shutterstock.com; cover, pp. 1-32 (wood background) Miro Novak/Shutterstock.com; cover, pp. 1-32 (old paper) Andrey_Kuzmin/Shutterstock.com; p. 5 (top) Miljan Mladenovic/Shutterstock.com; p. 5 (bottom) 3000ad/Shutterstock.com; p. 7 dibrova/Shutterstock.com; p. 9 (main) f11photo/Shutterstock.com; p. 9 (inset) Eblis/Shutterstock.com; p. 11 (top) © iStockphoto.com/EyeJoy; p. 11 (bottom) Jon Bilous/Shutterstock.com; p. 12 railway fx/Shutterstock.com; p. 13 (inset) © iStockphoto.com/Pgiam; pp. 14, 15 (inset) courtesy of the Library of Congress; p. 15 (main) © iStockphoto.com/ablokhin; p. 17 Songquan Deng/Shutterstock.com; p. 19 Nagel Photography/Shutterstock.com; p. 21 (top) ventdusud/Shutterstock.com; p. 21 (bottom) Jouko van der Kruijssen/Moment/Getty Images; p. 23 (top) John Seaton Callahan/Moment/Getty Images; p. 23 (bottom) Everett Historical/Shutterstock.com; p. 25 courtesy of NASA; p. 27 brytta/iStock Unreleased/Getty Images; p. 29 (top) Carolyn M Carpenter/Shutterstock.com; p. 29 (bottom) N8Allen/Shutterstock.com.

Printed in the United States of America

CPSIA compliance information: Batch #CS19GS: For further information contact Gareth Stevens, New York, New York at 1-800-542-2595.

CONTENTS

WORDS IN THE GLOSSARY APPEAR IN **BOLD** TYPE THE FIRST TIME THEY ARE USED IN THE TEXT.

WHAT IS A PRIMARY SOURCE?

Did you ever hear about something that happened and want to know all about it? It might be a good idea to look for a primary source! A primary source is a firsthand account, such as one given by a witness to an event. A good example is an interview from someone who actually saw the event. Photographs, video recordings, and newspapers can all be valuable primary sources. An object from long ago also can help you better understand how people lived then.

In this book, you'll learn about landmarks, a kind of primary source. Landmarks may be places or structures. Many landmarks are famous and attract many visitors each year. Visiting a landmark can give you much more information than just looking at a picture.

ANALYZE IT!

DO YOU THINK A PRIMARY SOURCE OR A SECONDARY SOURCE WOULD BE MORE **RELIABLE**?

SECONDARY SOURCES

WHILE PRIMARY SOURCES OFFER A FIRSTHAND ACCOUNT OF HISTORY, SECONDARY SOURCES OFFER MORE INFORMATION ABOUT IT. THEY MAY PROVIDE BACKGROUND OR USE FACTS FROM PRIMARY SOURCES TO EXPLAIN THINGS. SECONDARY SOURCES ARE OFTEN CREATED WELL AFTER THE EVENT IN QUESTION. A BOOK WRITTEN IN 2018 (OR 1818 OR 1918!) ABOUT THE AMERICAN REVOLUTION WOULD BE A SECONDARY SOURCE.

THE WHITE HOUSE

THE CAPITOL BUILDING

SINCE HISTORY HAS HAPPENED AT THE WHITE HOUSE AND THE CAPITOL BUILDING, BOTH ARE CONSIDERED LANDMARKS AND PRIMARY SOURCE LOCATIONS.

INDEPENDENCE HALL

What better example of a national landmark could there be than Independence Hall in Philadelphia? When construction began in 1732, many considered the hall the most ambitious public building in the colonies. This red brick building is, in many ways, the birthplace of the United States. It was here that courageous men representing the 13 colonies made the decision that those colonies would separate from Great Britain and form a new country.

The Continental Congress gave a committee of five men the task of writing a declaration about this decision. Thomas Jefferson wrote most of the declaration, with guidance from John Adams and Benjamin Franklin. Today, more than 600,000 people visit Independence Hall each year to see the meeting place where the Declaration of Independence was approved and signed.

ANALYZE IT!

WHY DO YOU THINK THE UNITED NATIONS EDUCATIONAL, SCIENTIFIC, AND CULTURAL ORGANIZATION (UNESCO) DECLARED INDEPENDENCE HALL A WORLD **HERITAGE** SITE?

THE CONSTITUTION OF THE UNITED STATES

IN 1787, JUST FOUR YEARS AFTER THE END OF THE AMERICAN REVOLUTION, IT BECAME CLEAR THAT A STRONG PLAN FOR GOVERNMENT WAS NEEDED IF THE UNITED STATES WAS GOING TO SURVIVE. REPRESENTATIVES FROM 12 OF THE 13 STATES CAME TO INDEPENDENCE HALL ONCE AGAIN. THE US CONSTITUTION WAS THE RESULT OF THAT MEETING.

BEFORE IT CAME TO BE CALLED INDEPENDENCE HALL, THE BUILDING IN PHILADELPHIA, PENNSYLVANIA, WAS THE PENNSYLVANIA STATE HOUSE.

THE GATEWAY TO THE WEST

Saint Louis, Missouri, is often considered the Gateway to the West. It's where Meriwether Lewis and William Clark began their journey into the Louisiana Purchase. The Oregon Trail and the Santa Fe Trail also began in Saint Louis.

The Gateway Arch in Saint Louis was built to honor Thomas Jefferson and Saint Louis's role in the westward expansion of the United States. The arch itself is a steel-and-concrete structure that's 630 feet (192 m) tall. It's the tallest man-made national monument in the United States. You must take a tram to get to the top of the monument.

ANALYZE IT!

HOW DO YOU THINK PEOPLE CONSTRUCTED THE GATEWAY ARCH?

From there, you can see the mighty Mississippi and Missouri Rivers. You can imagine what a journey into the still-wild western part of North America must have been like.

LOUISIANA PURCHASE

THOMAS JEFFERSON WANTED TO BUY THE PORT CITY OF NEW ORLEANS FROM FRANCE. HOWEVER, FRENCH EMPEROR NAPOLEON OFFERED THE UNITED STATES NOT ONLY NEW ORLEANS BUT ALSO ALL OF THE LOUISIANA TERRITORY FOR $15 MILLION. NO ONE AT THE TIME REALLY KNEW MUCH ABOUT THE TERRITORY. THAT'S WHY JEFFERSON SENT LEWIS AND CLARK TO EXPLORE THE AREA.

MUSEUM ENTRANCE

THE GATEWAY ARCH WAS COMPLETED IN 1965. IT INCLUDES AN INTERACTIVE MUSEUM WITH INFORMATION ABOUT NATIVE AMERICANS AND THE PIONEERS AND EXPLORERS WHO PASSED THROUGH MISSOURI ON THEIR WAY WEST.

FORT McHENRY

Visiting a historic fort can give you a similar point of view to the soldiers who fought there long ago. During the War of 1812, soldiers at Fort McHenry defended the harbor of Baltimore. In September 1814, British warships launched a 27-hour-long attack against the fort.

If you visit the star-shaped Fort McHenry, crouch down low against a wall. Imagine it's night, and British ships are firing cannonballs and rockets at the fort. The noise is intense. If you surrender, Baltimore will be at the mercy of the British forces, who will likely burn the city.

In the morning, the fort's commander replaced its small, battered flag with a huge 30-by-42-foot US flag! There was no surrender. The fort had survived the attack.

ANALYZE IT!

AFTER SUCH AN INTENSE ATTACK, WHAT DO YOU THINK BRITISH SAILORS THOUGHT WHEN THEY SAW THE HUGE AMERICAN FLAG RAISED AT FORT McHENRY?

THE STAR-SPANGLED BANNER

LAWYER FRANCIS SCOTT KEY WITNESSED THE ATTACK ON FORT MCHENRY. HE WAS ABOARD A BRITISH SHIP, WHERE HE WAS TRYING TO GET A PRISONER RELEASED. WHEN KEY SAW THE LARGE US FLAG THE NEXT MORNING, HE WAS INSPIRED TO WRITE THE POEM THAT BECAME "THE STAR-SPANGLED BANNER."

FORT McHENRY ENTRANCE

THE ORIGINAL FLAG FLOWN OVER FORT McHENRY IS CAREFULLY PRESERVED AND DISPLAYED AT THE SMITHSONIAN'S NATIONAL MUSEUM OF AMERICAN HISTORY IN WASHINGTON, DC.

THE ALAMO

The Alamo in San Antonio is one of the most visited sites in Texas. This landmark was originally a mission building constructed in the early 1700s. It became famous during the Texas Revolution. During the 1820s, Mexico invited some US citizens to settle in the Mexican state of Texas. However, by 1835, a new leader sent the Mexican army to kick the colonists out.

A citizen army formed to fight the much larger Mexican forces. In 1836, about 180 men from this Texan army occupied the building called the Alamo and refused to leave. The Mexican army killed all those men. This helped inspire the rest of the Texan army to win the revolution. Visiting today, you can imagine what the defenders of the Alamo faced during the ill-fated battle.

PEOPLE STILL FIND THE STORY OF THE ALAMO INSPIRING TODAY. WHY DO YOU THINK THIS IS?

TEXAS STATE FLAG

"REMEMBER THE ALAMO!"

THE CITIZENS OF TEXAS WERE OUTRAGED AT THE **MASSACRE** OF THE MEN AT THE ALAMO. TO THEM, THE MEN, LED BY WILLIAM B. TRAVIS AND JAMES BOWIE AND INCLUDING FRONTIERSMAN DAVY CROCKETT, WERE HEROES. "REMEMBER THE ALAMO!" BECAME A BATTLE CRY FOR AN INDEPENDENT TEXAS.

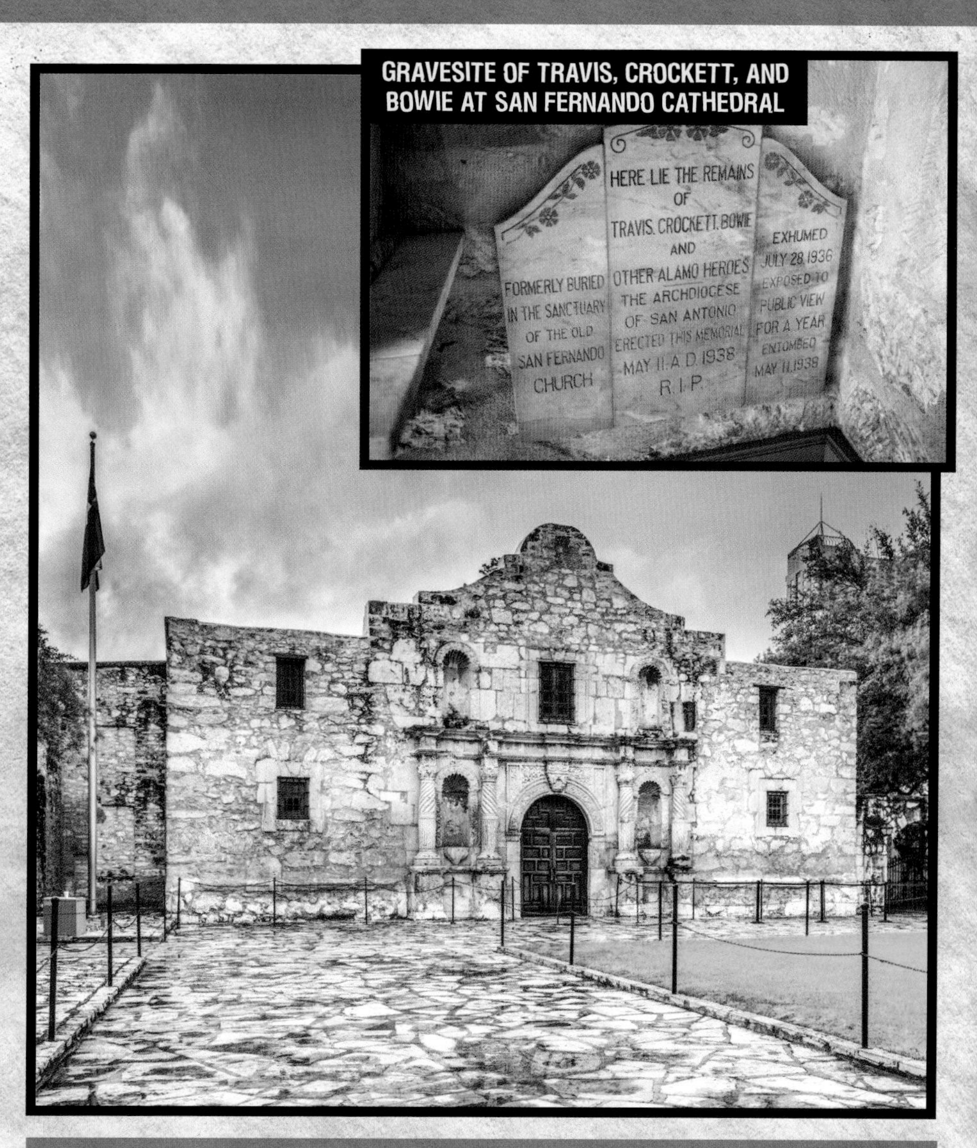

GRAVESITE OF TRAVIS, CROCKETT, AND BOWIE AT SAN FERNANDO CATHEDRAL

"ALAMO" IS SPANISH FOR "COTTONWOOD." THE BUILDING THAT BECAME KNOWN AS THE ALAMO WAS GIVEN THIS NAME BECAUSE IT STOOD IN A GROVE OF COTTONWOOD TREES.

GETTYSBURG

During the American Civil War, **Confederate** and Union forces met on July 1, 1863, near tiny Gettysburg, Pennsylvania. The three-day battle that started then was the turning point of the war.

Visiting this battlefield today, you still can get a feel for how large the battle was. The Union army had the better defensive position on Cemetery Ridge. Standing there, you can think about what it must have been like, looking out across the smoke-filled field as Confederate troops approached the Union positions. From the Confederate side, you see how far the troops in Pickett's Charge had to travel on that hot July day.

The Union won the Battle of Gettysburg, but by July 3, the battlefield was littered with more than 50,000 dead and wounded men.

LITTLE ROUND TOP
IN 1863

ANALYZE IT!

WHY DO YOU THINK THE UNION FORCES CHOSE TO OCCUPY THE HILL CALLED LITTLE ROUND TOP AT GETTYSBURG? HOW DID THIS POSITION HELP THEM?

THE GETTYSBURG ADDRESS

IN NOVEMBER 1863, THE GETTYSBURG BATTLEFIELD WAS DEDICATED AS A NATIONAL CEMETERY. EDWARD EVERETT GAVE THE MAIN ADDRESS, WHICH WAS MORE THAN TWO HOURS LONG. PRESIDENT ABRAHAM LINCOLN'S SPEECH WAS 272 WORDS, JUST 10 SENTENCES. TODAY, MANY PEOPLE CONSIDER IT TO BE THE GREATEST SPEECH IN AMERICAN HISTORY.

THE GETTYSBURG ADDRESS

DELIVERED BY ABRAHAM LINCOLN NOV. 19 1863

AT THE DEDICATION SERVICES ON THE BATTLE FIELD

Fourscore and seven years ago our fathers brought forth on this continent a new nation, conceived in liberty, and dedicated to the proposition that all men are created equal. * * * Now we are engaged in a great civil war, testing whether that nation, or any nation so conceived and so dedicated, can long endure. * * We are met on a great battle-field of that war. * We have come to dedicate a portion of that field as a final resting place for those who here gave their lives that that nation might live. * * It is altogether fitting and proper that we should do this. * * But in a larger sense we cannot dedicate, we cannot consecrate, we cannot hallow this ground. * The brave men, living and dead, who struggled here, have consecrated it far above our poor power to add or detract. The world will little note, nor long remember, what we say here, but it can never forget what they did here. * * It is for us, the living, rather to be dedicated here to the unfinished work which they who fought here have thus far so nobly advanced. It is rather for us to be here dedicated to the great task remaining before us, that from these honored dead we take increased devotion to that cause for which they gave the last full measure of devotion; * that we here highly resolve that these dead shall not have died in vain: that this nation, under God, shall have a new birth of freedom, and that the government of the people, by the people, and for the people, shall not perish from the earth

THE UNION TROOPS HELD A HILL CALLED LITTLE ROUND TOP AT THE BATTLE OF GETTYSBURG. IMAGINE TRYING TO ATTACK THIS HILL IN THE FACE OF UNION RIFLE FIRE.

ELLIS ISLAND

From 1892 to 1954, more than 12 million **immigrants** entered the United States through Ellis Island in Upper New York Bay to start a new life. Imagine leaving your homeland with just what you could carry and traveling across the ocean. After days of travel, you'd slowly begin to see New York City and the Statue of Liberty. Your ship would anchor, and ferries would begin taking passengers to Ellis Island. Carrying your bundles, you'd walk across the gangplank. As you joined a long line of people, the noise of people talking in many different languages might frighten you.

ANALYZE IT!

WHY DO YOU THINK THE UNITED STATES USED ELLIS ISLAND AS A SITE THROUGH WHICH IMMIGRANTS HAD TO PASS TO ENTER THE COUNTRY?

Visiting today, you can still see the castle-like building that people entered to begin the official process of arriving in the United States.

THE STATUE OF LIBERTY

THE STATUE OF LIBERTY WAS AN EAGERLY AWAITED SIGHT FOR MANY ARRIVING IMMIGRANTS. LOCATED ON LIBERTY ISLAND NEAR ELLIS ISLAND, THE STATUE OF LIBERTY WAS A GIFT FROM FRANCE IN 1885. IT ARRIVED IN 350 PIECES—SOME ASSEMBLY REQUIRED! LADY LIBERTY QUICKLY BECAME A SYMBOL OF PROMISE AND HOPE.

A JOURNEY TO ELLIS ISLAND TOOK ABOUT 7 TO 12 DAYS FROM EUROPE. THE FIRST IMMIGRANT TO GO THROUGH ELLIS ISLAND WAS 17-YEAR-OLD ANNIE MOORE FROM IRELAND.

MOUNT RUSHMORE

In the Black Hills of South Dakota, a national landmark is carved into a granite mountainside. Work started on the Mount Rushmore National Memorial in 1927 and finished in 1941. Artist Gutzon Borglum carved most of the memorial. He chose to carve the 60-foot-tall faces of four presidents—George Washington, Thomas Jefferson, Abraham Lincoln, and Theodore Roosevelt—because they represented important events in American history.

Washington was a hero of the American Revolution and the first president. Jefferson was the writer of the Declaration of Independence and the third president. Lincoln, the 16th president, guided the United States successfully through the Civil War and preserved the nation. Roosevelt was the country's 26th president. He's included for his role, or part, in developing the United States into a modern country.

ANALYZE IT!

IF YOU COULD CREATE A NATIONAL MONUMENT LIKE MOUNT RUSHMORE TODAY, WHICH PEOPLE WOULD YOU INCLUDE?

FATHER TO SON

GUTZON BORGLUM HAD BEEN WORKING ON A PROJECT SHOWING CONFEDERATE LEADERS AT STONE MOUNTAIN, GEORGIA. HOWEVER, HE LEFT THAT PROJECT AND BEGAN WORKING ON MOUNT RUSHMORE IN 1927. HE WORKED THE LAST 14 YEARS OF HIS LIFE ON THE MASSIVE PROJECT. AFTER HIS DEATH, HIS SON LINCOLN COMPLETED THE FINISHING TOUCHES.

NOTICE THE BIG PILE OF ROCK PIECES BELOW THE SCULPTURE. BORGLUM AND OTHER WORKERS SUFFERED LUNG PROBLEMS FROM BREATHING IN THE GRANITE DUST. HOW PRIMARY SOURCES CAME TO BE IS WORTH LEARNING ABOUT, TOO.

GOLDEN GATE BRIDGE

The Golden Gate Bridge in San Francisco, California, has been called one of the seven wonders of the modern world. The bridge, completed in 1937, has over 80,000 miles (128,747.5 km) of wire in its cables. The bridge features two main towers that soar 746 feet (227.4 m) into the sky. It was the longest **suspension bridge** in the world at the time it was completed—about 1.7 miles (2.7 km) long!

When construction on the bridge started in 1933, many people believed such a feat was impossible. They thought the water currents, winds, blinding fog, and earthquakes would stop its construction. Walking on the Golden Gate Bridge gives you a sense of wonder! You realize what people can build when they have **determination**.

ANALYZE IT!

WHAT ELSE WAS GOING ON IN THE UNITED STATES DURING THE TIME PEOPLE WERE BUILDING THE GOLDEN GATE BRIDGE? HOW DO YOU THINK THIS AFFECTED WHAT THE PUBLIC THOUGHT OF THE PROJECT?

INTERNATIONAL ORANGE

ORIGINALLY, THE US NAVY WANTED THE BRIDGE TO BE PAINTED BLACK AND YELLOW. INSTEAD, IT WAS PAINTED A COLOR CALLED "INTERNATIONAL ORANGE" SO IT WOULD BE EASIER TO SEE. TWENTY-EIGHT PAINTERS AND 13 IRONWORKERS WORK YEAR-ROUND TO MAINTAIN THE BRIDGE. ABOUT 2 BILLION VEHICLES HAVE CROSSED IT SINCE IT OPENED.

SOUTH TOWER

THE GOLDEN GATE BRIDGE CROSSES THE GOLDEN GATE STRAIT. IT CONNECTS SAN FRANCISCO TO MARIN COUNTY, CALIFORNIA.

PEARL HARBOR

Pearl Harbor, the headquarters of the US Pacific Fleet, is located on the island of Oahu in Hawaii. Its bay, separated from the ocean by a channel, has been deepened so very large naval ships can anchor there. When World War II began in 1939, the United States didn't become directly involved at first. However, on December 7, 1941, Japan launched a sneak attack on Pearl Harbor.

This attack sank or damaged about 20 ships, destroyed or damaged more than 300 aircraft, and killed more than 2,300 people. The next day, the US Congress declared war, joining the **Allies**, the nations that went on to victory in the war. Today, you can visit Pearl Harbor and imagine that peaceful Sunday morning when Japanese planes suddenly appeared.

ANALYZE IT!

WHY DO YOU THINK THE JAPANESE CHOSE TO ATTACK PEARL HARBOR? DID IT WORK? WHY OR WHY NOT?

THE USS *ARIZONA* MEMORIAL

THE USS *ARIZONA* MEMORIAL IS ONE OF THE MOST VISITED TOURIST STOPS IN HAWAII. THE *ARIZONA* SANK DURING THE ATTACK ON PEARL HARBOR AND WAS NEVER RAISED. MORE THAN 1,170 MEMBERS OF ITS CREW DIED. THE MEMORIAL ABOVE THE SHIP'S RESTING SITE WAS BUILT IN 1962. YOU CAN ONLY REACH IT BY BOAT.

PEARL HARBOR

USS *ARIZONA* BURNING ON DECEMBER 7, 1941

YOU CAN SEE THE USS *MISSOURI*, NOW A MUSEUM, AND FORD ISLAND IN THE TOP PHOTO OF PEARL HARBOR.

KENNEDY SPACE CENTER

When the Apollo 11 mission took off July 16, 1969, for the moon, it launched from Kennedy Space Center on Merritt Island, Florida. Every person who's set foot on the moon took off from this site on a Saturn V rocket.

Today, the Kennedy Space Center is one of 14 NASA visitor centers. You can see just how big a Saturn V rocket is. You can stand next to the space shuttle *Atlantis*, and you can touch a moon rock. You can see how rockets and space capsules became larger over the years as **technology** improved. You can take part in a program that lets you explore traveling to Mars. Would you like to have lunch with a real astronaut? At the Kennedy Space Center, you can!

ANALYZE IT!

THE PART OF THE EAST COAST AROUND THE KENNEDY SPACE CENTER IS CALLED THE SPACE COAST. THERE'S A REASON THE UNITED STATES LAUNCHES ROCKETS FROM THIS AREA. WHAT DO YOU THINK IT IS?

WE CHOOSE TO GO TO THE MOON

KENNEDY SPACE CENTER IS NAMED AFTER PRESIDENT JOHN F. KENNEDY. IN MAY 1961, KENNEDY SAID THAT THE UNITED STATES WOULD WORK TO LAND A MAN SAFELY ON THE MOON BY THE END OF THE DECADE. THIS GOAL WAS ACHIEVED WHEN THE APOLLO 11 MISSION LANDED ON THE MOON IN 1969.

MANY TOURS AT THE KENNEDY SPACE CENTER GO PAST THE VEHICLE ASSEMBLY BUILDING (VAB). THE VAB IS ONE OF THE BIGGEST BUILDINGS IN THE WORLD. IT'S 525 FEET (160 M) TALL AND 518 FEET (157.9 M) WIDE!

GROUND ZERO, NEW YORK CITY

September 11, 2001, was one of the most frightening and sad days in recent American history. A **terrorist** attack involving four airplanes killed nearly 3,000 people, destroyed the World Trade Center in Manhattan, New York City, and damaged the Pentagon in Washington, DC, among other buildings. Today, people can visit a memorial at the New York City site that marks the events of that day and honors those who were lost.

ANALYZE IT!

WHY DO YOU THINK THE NEW ONE WORLD TRADE CENTER WAS BUILT?

The 9/11 Memorial includes two pools located at the site of the two World Trade Center towers. Panels around the sides of the pools hold the names of the people who died in the attacks. The nearby 9/11 Museum contains **artifacts**, pictures, and videos that tell the story of that tragic day.

ONE WORLD TRADE CENTER

COMPLETED IN NOVEMBER 2014, ONE WORLD TRADE CENTER IS THE TALLEST BUILDING IN THE UNITED STATES AND THE SIXTH TALLEST BUILDING IN THE WORLD. IT'S ALSO SOMETIMES CALLED THE FREEDOM TOWER. VISITORS CAN TAKE AN ELEVATOR UP TO THE ONE WORLD OBSERVATORY, CLIMBING 102 STORIES IN 47 SECONDS.

THE 9/11 MEMORIAL IS A VERY **SOLEMN** PLACE. MANY PEOPLE WERE AFFECTED BY THE EVENTS OF SEPTEMBER 11, 2001.

ADVENTURES AWAIT YOU

Have you ever heard the expression "You had to be there?" The best way to learn about something is to experience it yourself. You may have the chance to see a primary source landmark in person. Every one of the landmarks in this book is a place you can actually visit.

Just imagine seeing the chair George Washington sat in during the Constitutional Convention at Independence Hall. Hum "The Star-Spangled Banner" as you look at Fort McHenry. Peek out the same window Davy Crockett may have looked out as he saw the approaching Mexican army at the Alamo. Follow in the footsteps of immigrants your own age at Ellis Island. Landmarks are primary sources that help us realize that history really happened!

ANALYZE IT!

THINK OF ONE OF YOUR FAVORITE TOPICS IN AMERICAN HISTORY. WHAT'S A RELATED LANDMARK YOU CAN VISIT?

HOMES OF THE PRESIDENTS

YOU CAN VISIT MANY OF THE HOMES OF FORMER US PRESIDENTS. MOUNT VERNON IN VIRGINIA WAS THE HOME OF GEORGE WASHINGTON. FRANKLIN D. ROOSEVELT LIVED IN SPRINGWOOD IN HYDE PARK, NEW YORK. THE HERMITAGE, WHICH BELONGED TO ANDREW JACKSON, IS JUST OUTSIDE NASHVILLE, TENNESSEE. WHERE WOULD YOU LIKE TO GO?

MOUNT VERNON

MONTICELLO

YOU CAN LEARN A LOT ABOUT THOMAS JEFFERSON BY VISITING HIS HOME, MONTICELLO, IN VIRGINIA.

GLOSSARY

Allies: the nations that banded together to oppose Germany, Italy, and Japan in World War II

artifact: something made by humans in the past

Confederate: having to do with the Confederate States of America during the American Civil War

determination: a quality that makes you continue to try doing something difficult

heritage: something that comes from past members of a family or group

immigrant: one who comes to a country to settle there

massacre: the killing of a large number of people, especially when they cannot defend themselves

reliable: able to be trusted

solemn: very serious

suspension bridge: a bridge with a road held by two or more cables, usually passing over towers and strongly anchored at the ends

technology: the way people do something using tools and the tools that they use

terrorist: one who uses violence and fear to challenge an authority

FOR MORE INFORMATION

BOOKS

King, David C. *Children's Encyclopedia of American History*. New York, NY: DK Publishing, 2014.

National Geographic Kids. *National Parks Guide USA: Centennial Edition*. Washington, DC: National Geographic, 2016.

National Geographic Society. *National Geographic Kids United States Atlas*. Washington, DC: National Geographic, 2017.

WEBSITES

Join the Journey
kennedyspacecenter.com
See what you can do and explore at the Kennedy Space Center.

9/11 Memorial and Museum
911memorial.org
Learn more about the events of September 11, 2001, and how they affected people of New York City and the United States as a whole.

The History Place Tourism Guide
historyplace.com/tourism/usa.htm
Explore links to more than 100 of America's favorite landmarks.

INDEX